STUDENT'S WORKBOOK

PRIMAL
HEALING

PRIMAL HEALING

FREEDOM FROM MOTHER WOUNDS

DR MARK STIBBE

Primal Healing – Freedom from Mother Wounds, Student's Workbook

Copyright © 2017 by Mark and Cherith Stibbe

Published by KINGDOM WRITING SOLUTIONS
Gargrave, North Yorkshire, BD23 3NG
www.kingdomwritingsolutions.org

ISBN-13: 978-1544178561

CONTENTS

ACKNOWLEDGEMENTS

There are a number of people I'd like to honor for their help in inspiring the growth and development of this workbook.

First of all, I'd like to thank Lois Gott. It was Lois who was the first person to identify the mother wound at the very core of my life. It was as a result of a morning with her and her husband Ken in the summer of 2014 that I started to think more deeply about the hurts that had been hiding in my shadow for such a long time.

Secondly, I want to thank my publisher and friend Malcolm Down. He has encouraged me to pursue the revelation in the pages that follow for a number of years. It's partly due to Malcolm that this course book has been written and I look forward to collaborating with him as my publisher on the book version.

Thirdly, I want to thank my counselor Lynn, a retired Christian psychotherapist and specialist in deep-rooted childhood pain, who helped me to navigate my way through the trauma of two phases of maternal abandonment in my childhood, and whose love and insight led to the development of this material on *primal healing*.

Fourthly, I'd like to thank those who have given me insights into the healing of mother wounds, from Juliette Coffey to Mark and Penny Carey. I am particularly thankful to Mark and Penny for pointing me in the direction of Dan Hughes' developments of John Bowlby's attachment theory.

Fifthly, I want to thank those who have given me space to trial this material in workshops in their communities - especially to Theresa Goode, Senior Leader of the New Dimension Apostolic Center in Rhode Island, and Adam and Rachel Graves, leaders of FreshFire Church, Manchester, UK.

Sixthly, I want to thank my wife Cherith for providing an environment of secure attachment - the perfect atmosphere in which to work through the issues of primal pain and primal healing. To Cherith I owe everything. If it wasn't for her, I would have never been able to research and write this material in a safe place.

Finally, I want to thank my adoptive Mum, Joy Stibbe, who went to be with the Lord just weeks before I finished this workbook, and whose love for me was unconditional throughout. Mum, your words at the lowest point of my life in October 2012 saved me: "Never forget, you are a much treasured son."

Thank you

And thank you El Shaddai, Lover of my soul, All-Sufficient One.

Dr Mark Stibbe

Session 1:
THE DIFFERENT KINDS OF MOTHERING

INTRODUCTION

The seven stages of childhood in the Hebrew Bible all revolve around mother

- Yeled (newborn infant), Isaiah 9:6

- Yonek (breast-feeding baby), Isaiah 11:8

- Olel (child who is now eating bread), Lamentations 4:4

- Gamal (weened child), Psalm 131:2

- Taph (little one, over two years old), Numbers 16:27

- Elem (youth), 1 Samuel 17:56

- Naar (youth who is free from childhood), Isaiah 40:30

Even before birth, the child's relationship with mother is critical

Oh yes, you shaped me first inside, then out;
  you formed me in my mother's womb.
Psalm 139:13 (The Message)

The mother-child bond is the primal relationship in our lives

> The impact of Mother is unparalleled. An attentive, capable, caring mother can help make up for many other handicaps, and the absence of such mothering is perhaps the greatest handicap of all
>
> Jasmin Lee Cori

In this first session we look at the continuum or spectrum of mothering styles

1. NOBLE MOTHERING

A noble mother is one who is attuned to the needs of her child all of the time

Anointed for Mothering . Children never insecure .

She meets the basic needs every child has for self-worth and security

The mother of Thomas Edison provides a supreme example

The noble mother builds a solid and secure foundation for her child's future

The Magi entered the house and saw the child in the arms of Mary, his mother. Overcome, they kneeled and worshiped him. Then they opened their luggage and presented gifts: gold, frankincense, myrrh.

Matthew 2:11

100% tuned to their children

2. NORMAL MOTHERING

Rebekah became pregnant. But the children tumbled and kicked inside her so much that she said, "If this is the way it's going to be, why go on living?"
Genesis 25:22

> Most mothers are what are classified as "good-enough mums"
>
> Dr Winnicott

> She is not going to always behave just right, but she has to know how to make it right when she misses
>
> Jasmin Lee Cori

30% tuned to their children

3. NEGATIVE MOTHERING

Ahaziah lived and ruled just like Ahab, his mother (Athaliah) training him in evil ways.

2 Chronicles 22:2-3

Four types of negative mothering have been spotted in contemporary Western culture:

- Helicopter Mothers -swoops in super controlling
- Tiger - conformity, strict, excellence academically.
- Attachment- demanding, unrealistic. Baby with Mum all time.
- Lazy - leaves child to do dangerous things etc.

We have expanded this list to seven types of negative mothering:

✱ 1. Dismissive _____ (of your existence, your feelings, your individuality)

✱ 2. Dictorial _____ (controlling, authoritarian, overly strict, disciplinarian)

✱ 3. Distant _____ (physically, emotionally, even to the point of desertion)

4. Desperate _____ "trophy Mum" (overly-invested in you succeeding)

✱ 5. Demeaning _____ (abusive, shame-inducing, either verbally or physically)

✱ 6. Disorientating (some days pleasant, other days aloof, other days cruel)

✱ 7. Dependant _____ (addicted, helpless, sick, turning you into the caretaker)

Some mothers grow good (enough) or grow bad over time while other mothers betray more than one of these negative mothering styles

For nearly two thousand years, the Church has been likened to a mother

Church is womb where new converts are birthed !

In what ways do the seven negative mothering styles correspond to your experiences of the Church?

1. D.E refusal to meet or speak to me/us

2. DE manipulation & control to obey.

3. Elders would not disobey DE leaving us rejected & deserted

4. Only wanted me to suceed with their agendas

5. Refusal to bring things into light causing negative assumptions

6. Started well disintegrated when God's plan was not their plan

7. N/A.

CONCLUSION

There is a gaping mother wound in many nations, including the UK

If you're Russian, you refer to "Mother Russia"

If you're German, you refer to "the Fatherland"

In the UK, we refer to the "Nanny State"

The recent James Bond movie, Skyfall, highlights the UK mother wound

We are a nation searching for the mother-like love of Father God

EXERCISE

Looking at your earliest years, in what ways were you subjected to negative mothering?

STYLE	SELDOM	SOMETIMES	OFTEN	ALWAYS
Dismissive (of your feelings)			✓	
Dictatorial (controlling and manipulative)		✓		
Distant (physically or emotionally)				✓
Desperate (over-investing in you)	✓			
Denigrating (shaming and abusive)				✓
Disorienting (nice one day, nasty the next)		✗		✓
Dependent (putting you in "caretaker" role)				✓

Did the situation change for the better or worse during your childhood, adolescence, young adulthood, until now?

Session 2:
WHAT TRUE MOTHER LOVE LOOKS LIKE

INTRODUCTION

You are he who took me out of the womb; you made me trust while on my mother's breasts
Psalm 22:9

We learn basic trust when we enjoy "secure attachment" at our mother's breasts

This is where our ability to receive and to give love is learned - from our mothers

Mother love or "secure attachment" is called *storge* love in ancient Greek

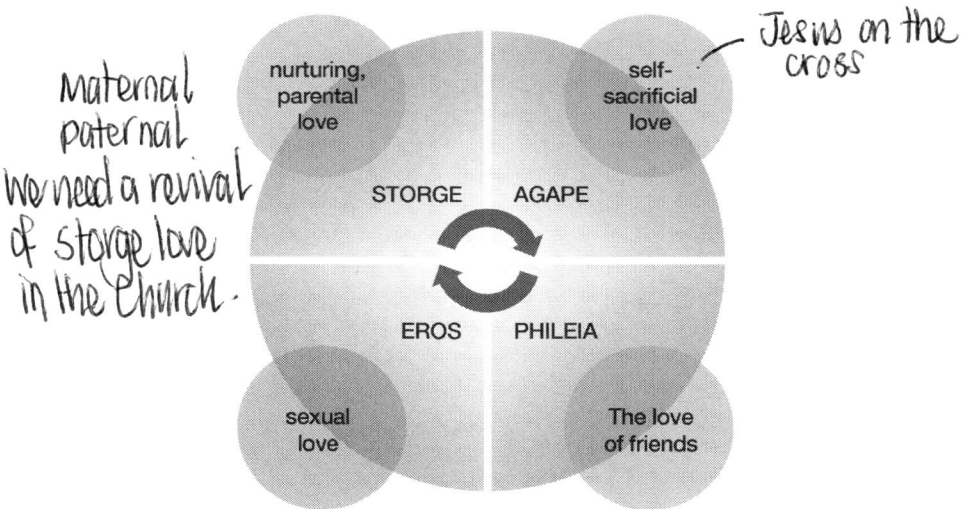

[Handwritten annotations: "Maternal paternal we need a revival of storge love in the church." and "Jesus on the cross"]

nurturing, parental love	self-sacrificial love
STORGE	AGAPE
EROS	PHILEIA
sexual love	The love of friends

Attachment begins in the first relationship of life, the relationship with Mother. This relationship begins early, even before birth, but is certainly shaped by the first few hours, weeks and months of life

Jasmin Lee Cori

There are three ways in which *storge* love is communicated from the Mom to her child

A) Eyes contact, mouth, touch

For a baby, the most painful experience of all seems to be not being able to get Mother's attention

Dr Sue Gerhardt

The Still Face experiment

B) Mouth - smiling etc

Hers is the first voice each of us hears, beginning with our existence in utero. From the moment we arrive in this life, her voice informs our sense of who we are

Peggy Streep

C)

The nurturing <u>touch</u> of a mother produces the following essential benefits:

- Enhances immune system
- Enhances growth of nervous system
- Helps us to feel loved, comforted & protected
- Decreases stress hormones

Nurturing, caring touch is an important building block in developing not only a sense of self but also a self that has value. It is such an essential need that babies deprived of touch often die

Jasmin Lee Cori

Overall, a mother communicates *storge* love through the following actions:

- looking at her child with love and not turning away with indifference or glaring with rage

- speaking softly and soothingly rather than harshly and coldly to her child

- touching, stroking, embracing, holding and kissing her child

Recently, Dan Hughes has developed the idea of secure attachment

He advocates helping children to grow through

P lay

A cceptance no matter what.

C uriosity

E mpathy

Jesus used this approach with his disciples!

Jesus demonstrated a mother-like love!

He created a safe environment in which his friends could grow in their attachment

In this and other ways, he released their creativity

He empowered them to seize their destiny

CONCLUSION

The benefits of the good enough mother's love are the following:

1.

The securely attached child develops a positive, healthy view of themselves and others

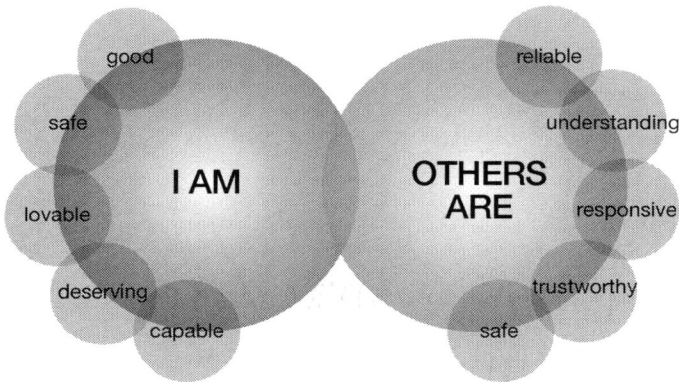

good
safe
I AM
lovable
deserving
capable

reliable
understanding
OTHERS ARE
responsive
trustworthy
safe

2.

For the young child, safety is being enveloped in an attuned, caring environment. It's not about locks on the doors but the sense that "Mommy will watch out for me. Mommy will remember me. I'm precious to her and she's not going to forget me." If Mommy is preoccupied, distracted, or annoyed and doesn't provide this, the child feels less safe. When you are dependent, security is feeling that the person you rely on is dependable

Jasmin Lee Cori

A mother's love gives her child a secure base for being creative

MOTHER LOVE ASSESSMENT EXERCISE

1. What memories do you have of your earliest years?

No close memories at all

- Do you have memories of close moments with your mother? *No*

- Were these moments of intimacy the exception or the rule?
Can't remember any intimacy

- How did your mother look at you when you were a child?
No memory

- What do you remember about the way your mother spoke to you? *No memory*

- Did you receive consistent, nurturing and caring touch from her? *NO.*

- Did you feel safe going to your mother in moments of need? *No*

- Was your mother emotionally empathetic, remote or annoyed?

2. What was your early relationship with your mother like?

Can't remember

3. What feelings does your early relationship with your mother evoke in you?

Fear because I can't remember

Session 3:
WHEN THE MOTHER
BOND IS BROKEN

INTRODUCTION

There is no pain like the pain of losing or missing out on a mother's *storge* love

This is *TRAUMA* and traumas can be either sudden or accumulative (DTD) *developmental trauma disorder happens over many years*

> Severe separations in early life leave emotional scars on the brain because they assault the essential human connection: the mother-child bond which teaches us that we are lovable; the mother-child bond that teaches us how to love. We cannot be whole human beings - indeed we may find it hard to be human - without the sustenance of this first attachment
>
> Judith Viorst

British psychiatrist John Bowlby and Attachment Theory is very important here

The five main points of Bowlby's theory

1. A child needs an attachment figure which is usually the mother

2. A secure attachment to Mom is essential in the first two years

3. There are long term consequences if this attachment is broken

4. The short-term results are protest, despair, detachment (DPD)

5. This primal attachment sets the blueprint for adult relationships

We now commonly talk about two kinds of attachment: secure and insecure

- reduced intelligence
- severe depression
* affectionless psychopathy - inability to show affection or emotion for the consequences of their actions. Shows no emotion!
- increased aggression.

27

The three types of *insecure* attachment are commonly known as

1. AVOIDANT ATTACHMENT

Mother's parenting style:

- No availability for the child, hardly there, rejection,
- absorbed in other things, distant, disengaged
- emotionally
-

Child's responses:

- Emotional distance
- Unable to explore safely
- Believes needs will not be met

Adult's consequences:

* - Avoids closeness & connection
- Becomes distant
- ✓ critical
- ✓ rigid / inflexible
- ✓ intolerant

2. AMBIVALENT ATTACHMENT

Mother's parenting style:

- Inconsistant

Child's responses:

- Anxious
- Insecure
- Angry
- Believes needs cannot be met

is one long journey punctuated by deliverance

Christian life - wonderful counselling punctuated by the wonderful counsellor.

Adult consequences:

- Anxious
- Insecure
- Controlling
- Blaming
- Erratic

3. DISORGANISED ATTACHMENT

Mother's parenting style: – _Domestic terrorism !_

- _Terrorising to ignoring - extremely inconsistant/abusive_

Child's responses

- _Depressed_
- _Powerless_

Adult consequences:

- _Chaotic lives_
- _Exhibit insensitivity_
- _Explosive & abusive themselves_
- _Untrusting even while craving security_

[Reader please note: we return to this at the end of audio session 4]

To get healed, we need to rewire our brains and renew our minds

This means renouncing the lies we believed because of broken attachments

We do this by bringing alignment between our thoughts and God's thoughts

You develop an orphan heart, abandonment & rejection when you have insecure attach

29

CONCLUSION

Believe these truths about your new true self as you grow in your healing

FALSE (OLD) SELF	TRUE (NEW) SELF IN CHRIST
Ashamed	Honored
Rejected	Accepted
Abandoned	Adopted
Undeserving	Deserving
Hopeless	Hopeful
Alone	Never alone
Incapable	Capable
Unexceptional	Unique
Fearful	Courageous
Detached	Engaged
Apprehensive	Contented
Frustrated	Fulfilled
Unreliable	Trustworthy
Untrusting	Trusting
Aggressive	Peace-loving
Insecure	Secure
Uncertain	Confident
Codependent	God-dependent
Neglected	Nurtured
Addicted	Free
Independent	Interdependent
Ugly	Beautiful
Failing	Successful
Poor	Prosperous
Fragmented	Whole
Condemning	Forgiving *of all people*
Unloving	Loving
Bad	Redeemed
Unlovable	Lovable

EXERCISE

List five lies you came to believe about yourself and replace them with five truths

LIES ABOUT MYSELF	TRUTHS ABOUT MYSELF
1 I'm rejected	I am loved by God
2 I won't be blessed	I am blessed
3	
4	
5	

Share what you have written

Now pray:

"Abba Father, El Shaddai, I confess the sin of agreeing to negative beliefs about myself. I repent of allowing these lies to affect my true identity in Christ. I decree that I am no longer ashamed and that I will no longer agree to any of these toxic beliefs. I choose to forgive my mother, and all others, for transmitting these lies and I release them from all my bitterness and judgment. I renounce these lies and I close the door of my heart to their influence over my life from this moment on. I demolish every orphan stronghold over my thinking and I choose to believe the truth about who I am in Christ. I pray these things in the mighty name of Jesus, my Strong Deliverer."

Spend the next 42 days (six weeks) saying, "I am not X", "I am Y"

Then thereafter every day decreeing only the positive, "I am Y!"

Session 4:

THE TELL TALE SIGNS OF PRIMAL PAIN

INTRODUCTION

So many people, even born again, well meaning, mature, Spirit-filled Christians, can be handicapped in the area of love and intimacy because they never learned to trust during the first two years of life and while on the mother's breast

Jack Frost

As with the orphan heart condition, there are *signs* and *symptoms* of the mother wound

SIGNS

External/Visible/Relational

SYMPTOMS

Internal/Invisible/Personal

There are internal *symptoms* of the primal wound that apply to both men and women - deprivation

- Loss of self esteem /shame
- Loss of trust
- Loss of boundaries
- Loss of joy /deep sadness
- Loss of feelings - emotionally disengaged

This is what Jack Frost means by being emotionally "handicapped"

Enemy exploits this to rob us - he comes to kill & destroy.

There are different (external) signs that we tend to see with each gender

1) WOMEN

What are the outward signs of the mother wound in a woman's behavior?

a) *Withdrawal in relationships particularly with women*

When women adopt a "fearful" or a "dismissive" stance with other women

b) *Care taking-disregards her own needs*

When women who took care of their mothers become co-dependents in adulthood

c) *Addictions etc.*

When women who lacked *storge* love resort to alcohol, relationships, food

d) *Self-harming*

When women try to mother themselves in ways that are self-destructive

Self-injury represents a frantic attempt by someone with low coping skills to 'mother herself'
Karen Conterio and Wendy Lader, *Bodily Harm*

This can also apply to eating disorders such as anorexia

Jesus goes to the root & in order to deal with the fruit

2) MEN

> As a culture, we tend to look at the mother's influence on the daughter and the father's effect on the son, thinking that each provides the mirror to either the feminine or masculine self. Does the legacy of an unloving mother spill over into a man's psyche and his ability to connect to women in ways that are unique? What happens to a man whose understanding of women is shaped by the first woman he encounters?
>
> Peggy Streep

What are some of the outward signs of the mother wound in a man's behavior?

a) Pornography, sexual addiction. *Serious disease in the Church!*

Sexual addiction in men can be evidence of the loss of *storge* love

b) Misogyny – hatred of women

Hatred of women in men can spring from a rage against the unloving mother

c) Delinquency – so many in prison had broken relationship with their mother

There is a clear link between the mother wound and juvenile delinquency (Bowlby)

d) Hostility

> By suppressing their sons' vigorous expression of spontaneous vulnerable feelings, mothers give boys the subliminal message that it is dangerous or shameful to manifest such feelings and that these feelings do not have an important place within their mother-son relationship
>
> William Pollack, *Real Boys*

CONCLUSION

The story of Moses gives us a vivid example of the effects of the primal wound

A) THE WOUND

A man from the family of Levi married a Levite woman. The woman became pregnant and had a son. She saw there was something special about him and hid him. She hid him for three months. When she couldn't hide him any longer she got a little basket-boat made of papyrus, waterproofed it with tar and pitch, and placed the child in it. Then she set it afloat in the reeds at the edge of the Nile

Exodus 3:1-3 (The Message)

B) THE SIGNS

Time passed. Moses grew up. One day he went and saw his brothers, saw all that hard labor. Then he saw an Egyptian hit a Hebrew—one of his relatives! He looked this way and then that; when he realized there was no one in sight, he killed the Egyptian and buried him in the sand. Rage and suppressed anger   40 years old   40 years in desert   80 burning bush

Exodus 2:11-12 (The Message)

The journey of healing for Moses was a long and hard one involving

a) Revelation

b) Re-wiring - renewing of our mind

Even then he still manifested the same sign of mother-loss when he was very old

The good news is that we live "the right side of the Cross" and have the Comforter

We enjoy the healing embrace of God's RUACH

EXERCISE

Complete the following two stem sentences

1. *In relation to my mother, I am angry that* ...She has not wanted me enough to be healed herself to enable her to be a good Mum.

2. *Beneath the anger, I feel* .... sadness that she has missed out on a loving relationship & I have not enjoyed a mum

LIST SOME THINGS FOR WHICH YOU NEED TO FORGIVE YOUR MOM

1. Manipulation and control
2. Rejection
3. Never having time for me
4. Selfishness
5. Avoidance of opportunities for us to experience breakthrough
6. Emotionally detatched from her family
7. Anger and aggression

Take off your shoes = Middle east : make yourself at home in my presence.

Exodus 3 & 4 indicates Moses orphan spirit
Leadership - influencing via modelling & communications.

Session 5:
A BLUEPRINT FOR ADULT RELATIONSHIPS

INTRODUCTION

A wise son makes a glad father, but a foolish son is the grief of his mother

Proverbs 10

Where is the mother of the prodigal son in the story in Luke 15?

a) Rembrandt's solution

b) Notice the ghostly figure of the mother in the corner of the room

'Look how many years I've stayed here serving you, never giving you one moment of grief, but have you ever thrown a party for me and my friends? Then this son of yours who has thrown away your money on whores shows up and you go all out with a feast!'

Luke 15:29-30

The mother-child relationship radically influences our adult relationships

This is the foundation upon which we will build all our future relationships

Secure attachment in childhood will lead to healthy adult relationships

Insecure attachments will often lead to the opposite

> The infant or child's experiences with her mother forge connections among the cells in the higher brain.... With secure attachment, we learn that "love means protection, caretaking and loyalty." With insecure attachments ... "love is suffocation"
>
> Peg Streep

There are two scenarios that often take place when mother love is missing

1) _____

Adults unconsciously seek out romantic relationships that mirror the mother-child pain

They form one attachment after another with partners who are

- Ambivalent

- Avoidant

- Disorganized

What was the message about love that you learned in your mother-child relationship?

- Love is

- Love is

- Love is

During the first years of life a child garners a deep impression of what love looks like

Our attachment in childhood influences our attachments in adulthood

CHILDHOOD ATTACHMENT	ADULT ATTACHMENT
Secure	Autonomous
Avoidant	Dismissive
Ambivalent	Preoccupied
Disorganized	Unresolved

Which adult attachment style best describes you?

2) _____

There are four common adult responses to deep-rooted childhood pain

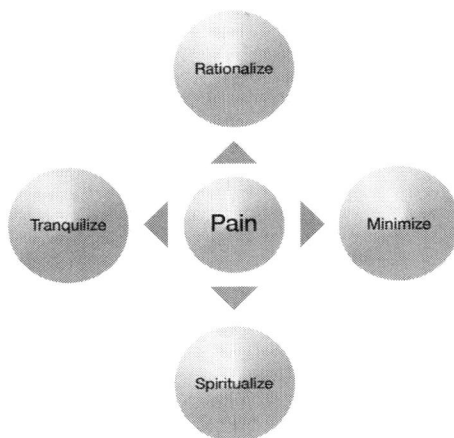

In the "replacement scenario", adults seek to tranquilize the lack or loss of *storge*

The most common response to maternal deprivation is substitute affections

Adults unconsciously seek out romantic relationships that mask the mother-child pain

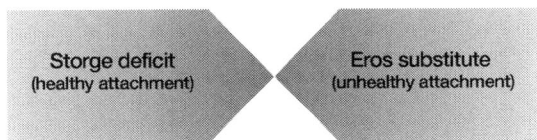

- Examples (Men)

- Examples (Women)

CONCLUSION

The mother-child relationship establishes the blueprint for all future relationships

Dan Hughes suggests eight keys for building healthy adult attachments

1. _____

2. _____

3. _____

4. _____

5. _____

6. _____

7. _____

8. _____

The mother-child relationship is like a dance (Robin Norwood)

We look for dance partners that replicate or replace that relationship

The only we can be free is by learning to dance with the Lord of the Dance!

EXERCISE

How has your relationship with Mom affected your adult relationships?

In what ways does insecure attachment in childhood negatively impact marriages?

Here is Denise Jordan, *The Forgotten Feminine*, p.104

"There are many men who try and get all of their 'mother needs' met through their wife's body. So many women have told me, "I feel like I am just like his mother. It is not about him and me in our marriage relationship. It is about him and his mother." She is not being loved by a bridegroom but rather a little boy with infantile needs, expressing themselves in a mature male body. It all manifests in the marriage bed, so she closes down emotionally and sexually, and he feels rejected and begins to seek other ways to satisfy his needs. The pattern is very prevalent and my heart breaks over it."

You may not be married, but you may have seen these patterns in relationships that surround you

How would understanding our mother-child attachment style help us to engage in healthier relationships/marriages?

Session 6:
FORGIVING AND HONORING YOUR MOM

INTRODUCTION

FAITH + FORGIVENESS = FREEDOM!

Matthew 6:14-15; Mark 11:25

What are the principles of forgiveness and honor when it comes to our moms?

1. THE FOUNDATION

Ephesians 4:32

The process of forgiving and honoring your mother must begin with revelation

"To understand all is to forgive all" (French proverb)

This foundational revelation comes in two ways

a) _____

Kathy's story

b) _____

Mark's story

2. THE PROCESS

Forgiveness is not saying, "What happened to me doesn't matter"

Forgiveness is the ability to recall hurtful things without them hurting you any more

The following steps need to be taken in the forgiveness process

Step 1: _____

Romans 12:19

Step 2: _____

Ephesians 4:26

Step 3: _____

Matthew 7:1-5

Step 4: _____

Colossians 3:13

Step 5: _____

1 Peter 3:9

3. THE CHALLENGE

Jesus calls us to forgive others from the heart (Matthew 18:35)

How are we to do that?

Forgiveness is not a feeling - it's a decision we make because we want to do what's right before God. It's a quality decision that won't be easy and it may take time to get through the process, depending on the severity of the offense

Joyce Meyer

When you make the decision to forgive, God's love gets right behind it

This enables you to move from the mind and the will to the heart

4. THE ENDGAME

The goal is to get to the place where you can honor your mother

Exodus 20:12

> Honor is the decision I make to give priceless value to another human being just because they are created in the image of God
>
> Dr John Trent, *The Gift of Honor*

There is a principle here: you can focus on the offence or you can focus on the fruit

Matthew 11:2-6

5. THE REWARD

"So you will live well and have a long life" (Ephesians 6:3, The Message)

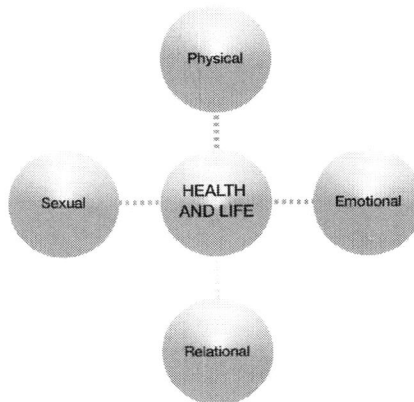

> To forgive is to set a prisoner free and discover that the prisoner was you
>
> Lewis B. Smedes

CONCLUSION

Children begin by loving their parents; after a time they judge them; rarely, if ever, do they forgive them

Oscar Wilde

We cannot experience primal healing until we forgive and honor our mothers

If, for nothing else, than the fact that she gave us life

The mother confession

THE HONOR EXERCISE

Use the word MOTHER as an acrostic and think of six things you can honor about her

M _____

O _____

T _____

H~~ard working~~

E _____

R ~~escuer~~

Now turn this into a prayer of thanksgiving

_____

_____

_____

_____

_____

_____

Session 7:
TERMINATING INHERITED PATTERNS

> Every mother contains her daughter in herself and every daughter her mother and every mother extends backwards into her mother and forwards into her daughter
>
> Carl Jung

There are inherited patterns of motherhood that bring life: 2 Timothy 1:5

There are inherited patterns of motherhood that bring death: Genesis 3:16 (See photo in Appendix 3)

Inherited mother wounds tend to get passed down in two ways

- Culture (the traditions of negative mothering in our particular sub-culture)

- Family (the patterns of negative mothering in our particular family tree)

We will look at both of these forms of oppression and then how to find freedom

1) _____

A particular culture can perpetuate harmful traditions of negative mothering

We can see how this happens in at least two particular cultures:

a) _____

Here are five stereotypes that can lead to oppression

Mammy - nurturing, family-oriented, self-sacrificial, church Mom

Siren - aggressive, uncaring, manipulative, promiscuous Mom

Sapphire - wise-cracking, stubborn, hateful Mom who has to be in charge

Oprah - career-focused Mom, not very nurturing, thick emotional exoskeleton

Welfare Queen - shuns work and passes bad habits and values on to her kids

Marilyn Yarbrough argued that these cultural stereotypes are rooted in slavery

The Good News is that Jesus sets the captives free!

b) _____

This is the mother who sends her children away to boarding school (at aged 8)

> "When she saw me crying before the beginning of one term she told me not to worry because I would soon learn to hide my feelings"
>
> Sarah Brown, former pupil of Cheltenham Ladies College

English mothers do this because of cultural tradition and addiction to status

But there is a toxic legacy to this mother wound, especially in marriage

Until mothers question their cultural traditions, they are simply perpetuated

2) _____

The second way we can inherit mother wounds is from our own family history

Negative and hurtful patterns of mothering can become generational

Our parents sinned and are no more,
* and now we're paying for the wrongs they did.*

Lamentations 5:7

This is true of negative and hurtful patterns of behavior in general

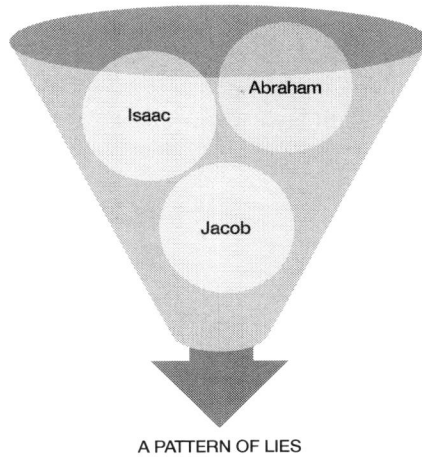

A PATTERN OF LIES

Genesis 20:2 (Abraham); Genesis 26:7 (Isaac); Genesis 27:32 (Jacob)

It is important to identify negative patterns relating to *motherhood* through

a) ....

b) ....

CONCLUSION

Do you remember the Scripture that says, "Cursed is everyone who hangs on a tree"? That is what happened when Jesus was nailed to the cross: He became a curse, and at the same time dissolved the curse. And now, because of that, the air is cleared

Galatians 3:13-14

Inherited patterns of negative mothering can become like a curse

We feel as if we are oppressed by something greater than ourselves

Here are seven keys to finding total freedom

Key 1: _____

Key 2: _____

Key 3: _____

Key 4: _____

Key 5: _____

Key 6: _____

Key 7: _____

It's time to cry freedom and say, "this far and no further!"

EXERCISE

Have a look at some of the common mother wounds passed down the generations

Do any of these apply to your family history?

- ✓ Abandonment
- ✓ Rejection
- ✓ Abuse
- ✓ Neglect
- ✓ Control
- ✓ Manipulation
- ✓ Withholding love
- ✓ Apathy
- ✓ Addiction
- ✓ Co-dependency
- ✓ Anger
- Smothering
- Over-investment
- Nagging
- ✓ Promiscuity
- ✓ Eating disorders
- Inconsistency
- ✓ Chaos
- Other

Session 8:
THE COMFORTING LOVE
OF EL SHADDAI

INTRODUCTION

Maybe what we have been calling this ministry of the Father's love has been a ministry of His motherly love

Jack Winter

A mother's love is a picture of the comforting love of God

Can a mother forget the infant at her breast, walk away from the baby she bore?
But even if mothers forget, I'd never forget you - never.

Isaiah 49:15

When a person suffers a mother wound, this sets them on a destructive path

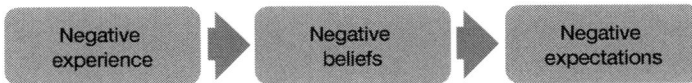

| Negative experience | → | Negative beliefs | → | Negative expectations |

To heal primal pain, we have to impact the feeling brain with a positive experience

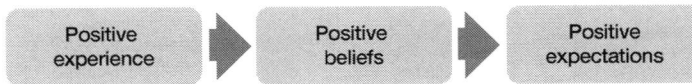

| Positive experience | → | Positive beliefs | → | Positive expectations |

The positive experience we need is an experience of the mother-like love of God

The most effective way to impact the limbic brain is through spiritual encounter

There is a great deal of openness to spiritual healing in mother wound therapy

The options offered fall easily into non-Biblical and Biblical categories

1. NON-BIBLICAL APPROACH

> Millions of people turn to Spirit for help in times of need.
>
> Jasmin Lee Cori

There are two main non-Biblical and "spiritual" approaches to primal healing

A. _____

> Through a devotional relationship with the Blessed Virgin Mary we find a mother's love that is complete and this love fulfills what was lacking in our own family dynamic
>
> Fr Dwight Longenecker, 'Pope Francis and the Mother Wound'

Weakness: Mary is a model of noble motherhood, not a divine mother

B. _____

Gaia – when the earth becomes a divine mother figure

God and his creation are believed to be one (pantheism)

Weaknesses: New Age spirituality worships the created not the Creator

WE ADVOCATE THE BIBLICAL APPROACH ONLY!

2. BIBLICAL APPROACH

The Bible teaches that God is both masculine and feminine - Genesis 1:27

Jesus expressed the maternal, feminine aspect of God's nature - Luke 13:34

The Holy Spirit has feminine overtones - Genesis 1:1 *(ruach)*

Rehem (womb) - *Rahamim* (compassion)

As a mother comforts her child, so I will comfort you
Isaiah 66:13

The way a father comforts his child and the way a mother does is different

> God did not satisfy Himself with proposing the example of a father, but in order to express His very strong affection, He chose to liken Himself to a mother, and calls His people not merely children, but the fruit of the womb, towards which there is usually a warmer affection.
>
> John Calvin, Commentary on Isaiah 66:13

Remember the two hands of Rembrandt's father in the Return of the Prodigal Son

A mother's love is a tender love while a father's love is a strong love

> The love of a mother is the veil of a softer light between the heart and the heavenly Father
>
> Samuel Taylor Coleridge

It is in God's nature to love us in a mother-like way

- _____

- _____

- _____

He is known as *El Shaddai*, the Strong-Breasted and All-Sufficient One

Through the Comforter, He releases nurturing, tender, soothing love

Only *El Shaddai* can make up the *storge* love deficit in our hearts

CONCLUSION

When we bring El Shaddai into the healing process, we can say with King David

Like a baby content in its mother's arms,
  my soul is a baby content.
Psalm 131:2

This comfort, once received, is to be given away to others with primal pain

He comes alongside us when we go through hard times, and before you know it, he brings us alongside someone else who is going through hard times so that we can be there for that person just as God was there for us.

2 Corinthians 1:3-4

The Church is meant to be in the world what the mother is called to be in the home

Denise Jordan

Let's be the vehicles of PHILOSTORGOS (Romans 12:10)

EXERCISE

As you receive a holy embrace, ask for a revelation of the mother-like love of God and a fulfillment of the promise in Isaiah 66:13

Let the nurturing, comforting love of God fill up the *storge* love deficit in your heart as you rest awhile in your stand-in mother's arms

A prayer:

El Shaddai, I come to you with an empty soul.

I have missed out on a mother's love

And I feel the primal pain of that so deeply.

By your Holy Spirit, the Comforter,

Please fill up the empty spaces of my soul;

Release your nurturing and tender love in me

And set me free to be a carrier of that mother love to others.

I ask this in the name of your Son, the Prince of Peace,

Amen

Session 9:
PUTTING HUMPTY TOGETHER AGAIN

INTRODUCTION

I went down to the potter's house, and I saw him working at the wheel. But the pot he was shaping from the clay was marred in his hands; so the potter formed it into another pot, shaping it as seemed best to him.

Jeremiah 18:3-4

In Abba's hands, we are healed in spirit, soul and body of our mother wounds (2 Thessalonians 5:23)

1. THE HEALING OF THE _____

a) GOD

In what ways has the mother wound affected your view of God?

b) CHURCH

If God is our Father, the Church is our mother
St Augustine

In what ways has the mother wound affected your view of the church?

c) PASTORS

In what ways has the mother wound affected your view of your pastors?

When we bring an end to projection, we bring an end to rejection

2. THE HEALING OF THE _____

The psyche or soul of a person comprises their thinking, feeling and choosing functions

When we experience insecure attachment, we experience soul fragmentation

a) _____

Have you shut down your emotions as a result of the loss of *storge* love?

Through El Shaddai's love, the limbic brain can be rewired and re-fired

b) _____

Did you experience *dissociation* as a result of being poorly mothered?

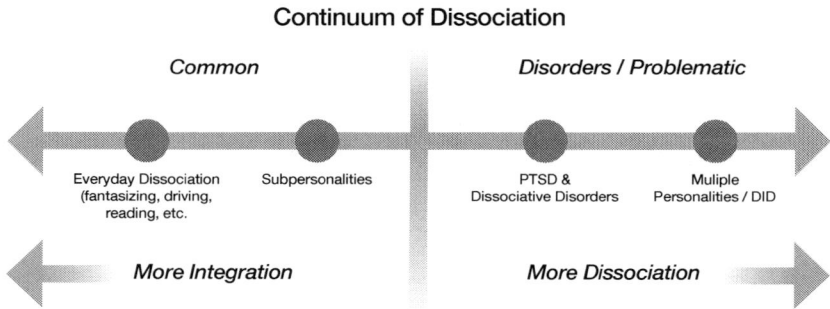

Continuum of Dissociation

Common		*Disorders / Problematic*	
Everyday Dissociation (fantasizing, driving, reading, etc.	Subpersonalities	PTSD & Dissociative Disorders	Muliple Personalities / DID

More Integration ← → *More Dissociation*

Bring those stuck parts of you into the throne room of El Shaddai

Let Him welcome, love, heal and reintegrate the fractured parts of your soul

3. THE HEALING OF THE _____

The primal wound doesn't just affect us in spirit and soul; it affects us physically

A mother kisses her infant's brain into life

The loss or lack of *storge* love can affect the development of a child's brain

The good news is that neuroscience teaches that our brains can be repaired

> It is nonetheless true - miraculous, even - that our own supremely flexible human brains can actually be "rewired" through new understanding
>
> Peggy Streep

CONCLUSION

All we are is messengers, errand runners from Jesus for you. It started when God said, "Light up the darkness!" and our lives filled up with light as we saw and understood God in the face of Christ, all bright and beautiful. If you only look at us, you might well miss the brightness. We carry this precious Message around in the unadorned clay pots of our ordinary lives. That's to prevent anyone from confusing God's incomparable power with us.

2 Corinthians 4:6-8

In the hands of El Shaddai, we are all examples of KINTSUGI art

The gold of the glory of God shines forth from broken not perfect vases

ON A DAILY BASIS, MAKE THIS
YOUR FAITH DECLARATION

GOD made my life complete
  when I placed all the pieces before him.
When I got my act together,
  he gave me a fresh start.
Now I'm alert to GOD's ways;
  I don't take God for granted.
Every day I review the ways he works;
  I try not to miss a trick.
I feel put back together,
  and I'm watching my step.
GOD rewrote the text of my life
  when I opened the book of my heart to his eyes.
Psalm 18 (The Message)

DECREE:

Father God, El Shaddai, I give you praise for putting my life back together when I placed all the pieces before you, that you have made my life complete and given me a fresh start, in Jesus' name, Amen.

What things are you are going to change in your life as a result of this course?

1

2

3

4

5

6

7

APPENDIX 1: Rembrandt's Painting of the Prodigal Son

Notice the mother in the background?

APPENDIX 2: BILL CLINTON, HIS MOTHER, AND MONICA LEWINSKY

APPENDIX 3: PEACHES GELDORF AND HER MOTHER

On Sunday April 6 2014, Peaches Geldof died of a drugs overdose ten times bigger than the one that killed her mother Paula Yates. She was just 25. Just a few hours before her death, she posted this photo of her younger self (left) and her mother (right) on social media, adding the caption: 'Me and my mum.' Her mother, Paula Yates, had died of a heroin overdose at the age of 41, when Peaches was 11.

APPENDIX 4: ADDICTIONS/CO-DEPENDENCY INVENTORIES (Dr Mark Stibbe)

ADDICTION/CATEGORY	ADDICTION/EXAMPLES
1. Substances	Food, alcohol, narcotics, tobacco, painkillers, sedatives, chocolate, sugar
2. Behaviors	Work, sport, shopping, gambling, thrills, exercise, fame, hoarding
3. Relationships	Sex, romance, approval, fantasizing, pornography, fetishes, obsessive love
4. Beliefs	Occultism, fundamentalism, perfectionism, Satanism, nihilism
5. Technologies	Gadgets, smart phones, tablets, Internet, TV, video games, texting, emails

CHARACTERISTICS OF THE CO-DEPENDENT PERSONALITY

A cultivation of a helping role in which you support and enable your partner's dysfunction

A tendency to do more of your fair share all of the time, often at the expense of your own interests

A replacement of an adult-to-adult relationship with a parent-to-child relationship with the addictive partner

A repeated pattern of clearing up your partner's messes and bearing their negative consequences for them

A commitment to stay in the relationship that is born from a need to be needed or a need for approval

Made in the USA
Columbia, SC
18 September 2018